"If you have been blessed by the biblical story of Shadrach, Meshach and Abednego, this book is for you. The inspiring story is presented in a creative, figurative, and allegorical form. You will read this amazing story and be left encouraged and deepened in your own faith in God who steps into the fire and delivers us."
Dr. Bryce Jessup, President Emeritus, William Jessup University

"The Bible is full of powerful stories. Dahlin makes those stories come alive! You'll think you were there, listening to their conversations, feeling their pain, and trusting their God."
Dr. Rob McCleland, President (ret.), John Maxwell Leadership Foundation, CEO of LeaderTribe.com.

"Mark Dahlin has opened the door to the missional conversation by choosing to reference Isaiah and Jeremiah. This story paints the picture of the "sending" nature of God's character and the mission of His Son to rescue fallen humanity. As God's people we have been invited into the *Missio Dei* (the Mission of God) that affirms the imprint of Christ's DNA on His church."
Cam Roxburgh, National Director for Forge Canada, Vice President of Missional Initiatives for North American Baptists.

The Babylonian Fire Scroll

Scroll

Brushstrokes of Grace

Splashes of Glory

Mark Dahlin

Illustrated by Kate Vaughn

DR

Dead Reckoning Publishing House

DeadReckoningMinistries.com

Babylonian Fire Scroll: Brushstrokes of Grace Splashes of Glory
Copyright © 2016 by Mark Dahlin
Published by Dead Reckoning
                Sacramento CA 95621

Illustrations by Kate Vaughn

First Printing 2016
Printed in the United States of America

                        ISBN 0692796993
                        ISBN 978-0692796993

DEDICATION

I want to dedicate this small book to all those around me who make me better, most importantly to my incredibly talented wife—Kerry who is a true Proverbs 31 woman and to my amazingly talented children.

CONTENTS

ACKNOWLEDGMENTS

Thank you heavenly Father for your endless supply of lavish grace. Thank you to my Roseville critique group for your input. To Ruth Morse, Caryl Sheehan, and Grace Knight for your spit polish and to all the people who have encouraged me to put this story in print format.

Thank you Kate Vaughn for taking on the task of using your gifts and talents for the whimsical and beautiful illustrations that has made this book come alive.

INTRODUCTION

This story is written in the spirit of the Rabbinic Midrash tradition. The Midrash was an ancient form of rabbinical exposition of stories found in the Old Testament. They viewed the creative retelling of the Bible stories as praiseworthy attempts to familiarize people in a way that provided commentary about the sacred text. This custom was a basis for practical application and observance, especially since they were so far removed from the context of the original events.

Midrashim (plural) are not literal interpretations, but figurative and allegorical, written with the expressed purpose of confirming the truths of the Bible to encourage a manner of faith and practice for the hearers.

Although there is no such Babylonian Fire Scroll, I pray this rabbinic-style of artistic adaptation will be a blessing, a challenge and an encouragement to your faith. This modern retelling highlights the brushstrokes embedded in the Hebrew language so that the reader might be astonished by the colorful hues of God's grace and the splashes of His glory.

Part 1

FIRE

CHAPTER 1

THE NINE

Angry mobs were herded like cattle into a dust-bowl under the veil of darkness. Tension escalated as captives grumbled in protest. Yet, of all the nations under Nebuchadnezzar's rule, the Jews proved to be most difficult to control. In the early morning, the king's plan was contingent upon getting his subjects onto the plain before daybreak.

Anarchy was at its tipping point. Brusque guards hastily pushed the prisoners along the mile-long path leading the anxious hordes out of the city. Tempers flared and chaos ensued as Nebuchadnezzar employed the full force of his military to maintain the fragile order of the restless multitudes.

The faint cry of a small child which had been torn from a mother's grip went completely unnoticed. Screaming, the Scythian mother was quickly shoved along by one of the Babylonian guards.

A Jew—a Jew who will be known simply as Number Four— heard the mother's anguished plea and fought his way back through the crowds. He saw the terror in her eyes and knew something was desperately wrong. In the confusion of anxiety and fear, no one was able to hear the cry of the abandoned child who wandered dangerously into the heavy foot-traffic. Number Four trained his ear to the weeping of the infant boy and reached him just as he was about to be trampled by one of the Babylonian soldiers. Number Four threw himself over the child and took upon himself the crushing blow of the inattentive guard.

Painfully standing to this feet, Number Four tenderly caressed the baby and returned it to its mother.

"Thank you," said the Scythian woman in broken Babylonian, "and thank Nebo."

"No," said Number Four. "Nebo had nothing to do with this. Thank the One true God of heaven and earth…the God of Israel."

Grimacing with pain, Number Four brushed himself off and rejoined his group on the plain outside the lush city of Babylon.

———— ✶ ————

Long shadows danced behind the countless bodies that moved like wheat swaying in the breeze. The warm vapor of anxious breath mixed in the cool morning air to create a misty haze above the heads of those forced to assemble.

The sun followed its path in the canopy of the sky as red hues morphed into bright yellow light heating the arid valley. As the rays intensified and burst over the distant mountaintops, bright beams hit the statue and made the monstrous idol look like it had been awakened. Like the face of a god descending from heaven, the image pierced the low-hanging fog.

Standing at that exact moment, Nebuchadnezzar raised his arms into the air as if commanding the idol to come alive.

Haha. "Tell me that wasn't calculated and planned out by his stargazers," whispered one of the captive Jews.

"Yes. Cunning more than coincidence, I'd say."

As if awed by the radiance of the towering edifice, multitudes stood at a distance and marveled.

"I guess His Majesty is getting what he wanted," said Azariah.

A heathen from the east was overheard saying, "Surely this is God himself." Those words were enough to cause many to fall prostrate before the imposing golden figure.

One of those among the favored group of Jews who had been schooled in the Chaldean language said, "Babylon means 'The gate of god.' Certainly, none of us from Judah is going to fall for this blasphemy."

Number Four laughed, then said, "Gate of God," as if mocking how unlikely this was for a place like Babylon.

"This is not about bowing to a lifeless statue. This is about Nebuchadnezzar's ambition for world domination and control," murmured one of the high ranking Jews near the front. "I think he's attempting to use this dedication ceremony to lord it over us so our people would forget the One True God of Israel."

"This brazen idolatry is blasphemous," said one of the finely dressed and exclusive Jews assembled not far from the foot of the throne.

With the commanding effigy towering into the sky, Number Four looked over his shoulder and saw that not one of the Jews of lower social rank had bowed. "We will worship Yahweh only, and none of us would ever serve a lifeless idol," he said. "Never."

Nebuchadnezzar's empire expanded outward to nations he had conquered and the capital city included the vast number of those brought back into exile. Many of his advisors and officials were of different races and nationalities, including the people from Jerusalem in his Egyptian campaign. This particular group of Jews was a privileged class. As priests and princes from the house of King Jehoiakim, they have been set apart to govern certain affairs of the provinces of Babylon.

Because of their close proximity, they could hear some of the king's conversations with his Chaldean satraps and magistrates.

One of the prominent Jews protested, "This dedication ceremony is nothing more than a test—"

"This has nothing to do with his god," interrupted a brother Jew. "This spectacle is only a means to sift out any disloyalty."

"God forbid that any Jew should give in and bow. Surely none in our group ever will," said Number Four, loud enough to be heard by the Chaldean officials near the king. Turning to the countless Jews who stood behind he pointed to the statue and said, "I only pray that none of the other Jews would give in by surrendering to this…this…this graven image."

A chief official among Nebuchadnezzar's astrologers and a junior advisor approached the advantaged class of Jews. "It is only for Belshazzar's sake that the King tolerates you at all. His Majesty had Belshazzar, the one you call 'Daniel,' stay back at the court so he could not be here to intercede for you," he said, smirking.

"We will break you," said the other one with him to a small group of those up front who were most vocal in their taunts.

A grin cut across the face of the senior official as he walked up to Azariah and surveyed him from head to toe. "Just look at yourself, standing here in the finest Babylonian attire. It is Nebuchadnezzar's plan to make you forget your past…your customs…your god, and to give you a new identity. Ha!" he laughed throwing his head back.

The subordinate officer laughed along with him. "As for you, Azariah," he said poking him in the chest, "Your Jewish name means 'Jehovah has helped' but that can no longer be said of you. Your God cannot save you now. You will now serve this god we call Nebo. Why do you think we gave you the new name—Abed-Nego?" Laughing, he pushed Abednego and said, "Which means, 'the servant of Nebo.' We will make you like us or you will be nothing at all."

Glancing into the eyes of each Jew as he slowly walked past, the officer further taunted them, "We will wring the Hebraism out of you. By bowing to the golden statue," he said lifting an eyebrow, "Nebuchadnezzar will be your god."

"Never," shouted Number Four again.

"We shall see about that," said the second officer while scowling at Number Four.

The arid plain outside the city was flat. Not far from the colossal image Nebuchadnezzar had a mound built to elevate his throne for this auspicious occasion. Off at a safe distance, a second mound was created for the fire smelt that refined the gold used for the enormous statue. Messengers had been scattered into the crowd to proclaim the king's decree. They warned everyone that at the sound of instruments all subjects were commanded to bow down before Babylon's god. "By his Majesty's decree…whoever does not fall down and worship will immediately be thrown into a blazing furnace."

"God of heaven deliver us," cried out Hananiah. It was only when the messengers announced the penalty for disobedience that any of the Jews, whether nobility, priest or peasant understood the full intent of Nebuchadnezzar's wicked scheme.

Rubbing his hands together with a look of delight on his face, a magistrate worked his way to get close to the special group of Jews. "Only fitting, don't you think? Perhaps, divine paradox might be a better way of describing," he said smirking, "how you will be executed in the same fire that produced our god. Ha…did you honestly believe we thought the king's command would be incentive enough for you to bow? No, we were not going to leave that to chance, you fools. The king knew that the other nations would bow but decided to give you stubborn Jews more motivation."

The chatter from the Jews in the front was speculation on this very thing. They began to tell each other how the king anticipated the heathen captives from other nations would bow to just about anything. They concluded this entire event was nothing more than a deceptive ploy to bend the will of the obstinate children of Israel from Jerusalem. "Obstinate" was a word the king often used to describe them and had thrown that term in their face quite a bit during their three years of indoctrination.

"I'm worried that our people might not be as *obstinate* as he thinks we are. Brothers, I have a terrible feeling that the less privileged Jews might bow."

"No matter what those other Jews do, please make a vow that not one of us among the priests and princes of king Jehoiakim will bow," pleaded a member of the superior cadre.

"I swear to you I will not." Number Four said loudly, as if hoping his booming voice would cause those around him to make a similar pledge.

Hearing the resentment of those up front, Nebuchadnezzar furrowed his brow and scowled at Hananiah. He had heard the overt murmurs of those swearing not to bow.

The king snapped his fingers and pointed in their direction. Two commanding officers immediately dispatched guards who came and infiltrated the group. They looked too ready as if they knew what to do. It affirmed the king had anticipated this.

"The trial begins," said a Jew near the front. "He thinks we're fooled by this pretentious ploy. Stand strong brothers. This is about purging his administration of any he can prove to be disloyal."

"He thinks he will replace God as the One who has all authority and power—"

"And so foolish to think that he could win this contest of wills."

"This is a not a battle he can win," said Number Four.

"Our God brought us through the Red Sea," said Azariah. "He will see us through this."

The day became scorching as the sun climbed high overhead—and with the final preparations complete, Nebuchadnezzar leaned over to one of his provincial officials. In a voice loud enough for the Jews in front to hear, he spoke past his advisor and said, "Who or what could save any of them now?" Laughing, he looked down and intently studied his palms. "Not even the god I created has the power I hold in my hands."

"He thinks we're ignorant. This is not about bowing to his god. Bowing to his idol is like surrendering to him as supreme ruler."

Standing to his feet he thumped his chest with a closed fist and looked directly at the group while speaking to his Babylonian advisors. "Their pitiful god couldn't even save them when I surrounded their sacred city." Laughing like a drunkard, the rich adornment of the king's jewelry chimed as he raised his hand—the signal for the musicians to play.

The sound of the lyre, harp, flute, horn and music of all kinds could be heard from the hundreds of instrumentalists who had been positioned around the gathered nations.

"This is it," said Azariah. "He has commenced his evil conspiracy."

"This is the test of our faith," said Number Four, extending his elbows to his neighbors. "Lock arms with me, brothers."

After the music sounded, those with locked arms were not surprised to see the rest of the multitudes from other nations bow down like a wave rolling across the open sea headed in their direction. An unsettling murmur among some of the peasant Jews behind also carried forward. A conflict arose between those who voiced their readiness to join the swell of bodies bowing down and the faithful Jews who rebuked them by reminding them of the law.

Mishael turned around with such force that he knocked the Jew next to him off balance. "No other gods!" he shouted above the noise.

Steadying himself. Number Four hollered to those around him. "Do not give in. Stay on your feet!"

Though close enough to watch the guards stoke the furnace, Nebuchadnezzar and his advisors, magistrates and astrologers were far enough away to not feel its searing heat. The smelt sparked and sprayed red-hot embers that glowed like shooting stars in the black backdrop of the billowing smoke. The sight and smell were terrifying incentives to bow.

"This…this…this statue…this god, Nebo, is just one god of many to the other nations," said one of the privileged Jews pointing to the despised golden edifice.

"What do they have to lose should they surrender?" said another, pointing to the carpet of bodies bent low to the ground. "We are not like them. We alone have the law. It was given to us by God through his servant Moses. The first commandment is that He alone is God and we should have no other god before Him. The second is that we should not bow or worship any form or graven image."

"Please, Lord, protect your people," Hananiah said. "Lord, help us stand...*oomph*—" cut off mid-sentence by a sharp elbow-blow to the ribs, Hananiah looked in the direction of the newest commotion to see Jews falling to their knees.

"Remember what happened at Marah. Do not give into temptation like our fathers did that day at Massah in the desert. Do not bow. Have faith, brothers. Do not let your hearts go astray," Number Four pleaded as if heartbroken.

As Nebuchadnezzar's guards pressed in on the Jews, the reality of certain death caused more to fall shamefully to their knees.

"It doesn't matter. Desperation or cowardice are counted the same—faithlessness and idolatry. Do not test God."

"It seems our destiny is in his hands," said another Jew, retreating to his knees.

Hananiah shouted, "If you bow, your destiny will be in his hands." He motioned with his head to the king. "But mine will be in the hands of the God whom I serve."

With no more veiled intentions, the king boldly gestured to the death chamber and laughed while telling the astrologers nearest him, "What kind of choice have I given them?"

Joining the king's laughter, those closest to him glared in the direction of the unyielding sect in front. "Your Majesty, you have them in your hand. Now crush the infidels in your fist."

"Look at them. They seem so pleased with themselves," said one of the Jews pulling the Babylonian turban from his head and throwing it to the ground.

"Like they have tasted victory."

"We'll see about that," said Number Four.

One brother knelt while echoing the words of the king. "What kind of choice has he given us?"

Those spineless words obviously incited greater fear as more followed him to their knees.

"Who will stand with me? *I…will…stand…*though none other stands with me." Number Four said straightening his posture like a pillar in the temple of Jerusalem.

Nebuchadnezzar was not so blind that he couldn't see what was taking place in front of him. Yet, his astrologers came forward. "May the king live forever," they said pointing out the small group still standing. From the look on their faces they seemed to delight in informing the king of the small-scale rebellion.

The king's eyebrows knit together and his face was as red as the fire. He leaped from his throne and threw his arms into the air. In a fit of rage, he ordered his guards to move in upon the few left standing.

Out of the thousands—twelve stood.

With swords drawn, the guards approached. One of the princes bowed, saying, "If we get thrown into the fire what good are we to God anyway?"

"Excuses," said Number Four. "As if there was any *good* reason to bow—"

"The statue is nothing," loudly interrupted a Jew behind him. "Save yourselves by bowing and praying to God. God can see into our heart."

"God does know your heart, but now you have exposed it to the rest of us to see," Mishael shouted. "I will not obey Him with my lips only, but will obey God with my very life, if that is what it comes to."

Halfway through Number Four's all-to-eager, "Amen," two more Jews in the prestigious group kneeled.

Only nine stood. Nine, brave and faithful.

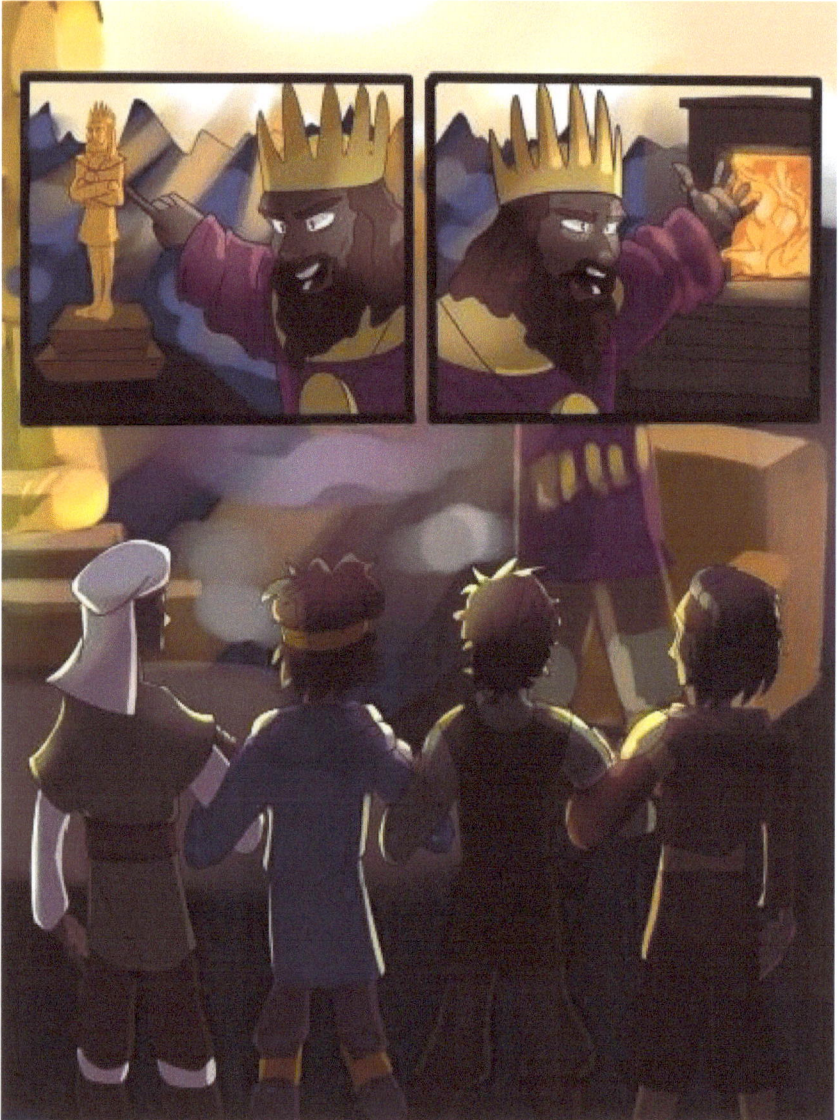

CHAPTER 2

THE FOUR

As the sound of the instruments began to wane, Mishael led the nine in reciting the law, "Thou shalt not make unto thee any graven image. Thou shalt not bow down thyself to them or serve them."

The death chamber gave up a loud crack, startling one of the approaching guards. The spewing shower of sparks was a visible, terrifying reminder of the consequences. It was as though the furnace hungrily begged for human flesh. The standing Jews darted glances at one another and huddled closer as if the awareness of imminent death struck a fearful chord.

Another Jew of nobility made a pious sounding plea, "I am a believer in the one true God of Israel, but can God save us from this?" He and another brother bowed before the giant idol.

Seven stood.

"Stand, you cowards," Number Four yelled over his shoulder with slight uncertainty in his voice.

The fact that seven still stood among the multitudes appeared to be enough to drive Nebuchadnezzar to the brink of madness. In a violent gesture of his hand he motioned for the guards to bring the seven condemned men before his throne.

Number Seven crumbled under the pressure and pleaded with the others to join him. "Save yourselves. There's still time. It's not too late."

Without flinching, Azariah said, "My God is able. This is our time."

Several more guards forcefully maneuvered through the bodies and grabbed the faithful remnant who had arms locked together. Number Six pulled away from the group, knelt and said, "If we don't bow down…we will be playing into the hands of the jealous Chaldeans who are just using us to further their cause."

The fifth one standing said, "Would God have brought us this far just to die? Certainly, by complying and keeping our high offices, we would be better able to help God's people."

Unable to hold back tears, Hananiah dropped his head and pleaded as if not caring whether anyone heard, "I would rather serve God in death than worship an idol in life."

Only four remained.

"If these two bow, I will stand with you, Hananiah," Number Four said earnestly.

Brandishing a sword, one of the sentinels grabbed Mishael by the wrist tearing him from the arm of Number Four who was left standing all by himself.

Cracking under the pressure. "It's only a statue…j…just a…m…meaningless idol. Why not bow down while praying and praising our God?" said Number Four, hastily joining the others, genuflecting to the king and his imitation god.

And then there were three.

Part 2

FAITHFULNESS

CHAPTER 3

THE THREE

The magistrate who had mocked the Jews earlier approached the king slowly and fell to his knees before him. He feigned great humility. "Oh, great king live forever, it is three from the tribe of Judah, as you expected—Hananiah, Mishael and Azariah. The favored of all your officers who were given the Babylonian names Shadrach, Meshach and Abednego. Your Majesty, they refuse to obey your command."

"How dare they defy me," screamed Nebuchadnezzar, "after all I've done for them? I clothed them, educated them and gave them high positions within my court. Betrayal!" Spitting on the ground in a Chaldean gesture of disowning a child, he said. "Bring me the Hebrew dogs." He motioned so violently that the crown fell from his head. "Leave it," he said to an eager advisor as if he had more important matters at hand.

Though the three final holdouts gave little resistance they were forcibly dragged before Nebuchadnezzar. The hulking sentinels acted like they had to impress the king and grabbed the men by their shoulders, yanked them straight, and squared them to the emperor.

Brows furrowed, sticky white saliva lathered at the corners of the king's mouth. "Shadrach, Meshach and Abednego, is it true that you do not serve my gods nor worship the gold statue I have set up?" His face was almost as red as the glowing embers in the furnace. "In a moment you will again hear the sound of the horns and flutes and all the other musical instruments. The only hope you have is to bow down and worship," he said looking directly at them while pointing to the furnace.

His face twisted as if pained, "But if you do not worship it, you will immediately be thrown into the blazing furnace." With deep breaths, nostrils flaring, he paused as if composing himself and then challenged the three whom he previously held in high respect, "What god will be able to save you from my power then?"

There was no response from the three.

"Stand down," Nebuchadnezzar said to the guards who immediately released their grip and stepped back from the prisoners.

He thumped his chest, picked up his jeweled crown and held it high in the air. It was an obvious display to let everyone kneeling know that this defiance was a challenge to his sovereign reign and would not to be tolerated.

"His pride has been hurt," Number Four said to the Jews bowing near him.

"You have seen my power when I conquered your land and took your people as slaves. Yet, I did not treat you as slaves like I did the rest of them or like the multitudes too numerous to count who are bowed behind you. I chose you and included you as if you belonged to my house. I acted kindly towards you and gave you high positions of honor. How dare you do this to me?"

Without so much as a flinch, Shadrach, Meshach and Abednego looked straight into the king's eyes. Shadrach said, "That is true Your Majesty. We don't want you to feel like this is a betrayal—"

"Betrayal? What do you think this makes me look like?" he shouted. "This is treason and you've given me no other recourse!"

"Nebuchadnezzar, we do not need to defend ourselves to you. If you throw us into the blazing fire, the God we serve is able to save us from the furnace."

Meshach took a small step forward, standing partially in front of Shadrach. "He will save us from your power, O King."

The trial paused when those near the front reacted to a loud crack as the furnace belched out hot embers.

Number Four shook his head and whispered to those close around him, "They should have knelt with me when I pleaded with them. Think how much more we can do for God by choosing to stay alive."

"By becoming more like the Babylonians we can turn more hearts to worship God," said Number Five.

"Yes," said Number Six. "We need to assimilate more into their culture if we are to be any good to God."

Up front, Abednego boldly stepped forward, closer to Nebuchadnezzar, "But even if God does not save us, we want you, O king, to know this: We will not serve your gods or worship the gold statue you have set up," he said loud enough for the Jews kneeling near the front to hear.

Raising both hands as if questioning what to do next, Nebuchadnezzar turned right and left, back and forth to the advisors and astrologers next to him. Licking the white sticky substance from the corners of his mouth, Nebuchadnezzar finished by wiping his face with the back of his hand. "I told my closest advisors," he said pointing to those on either side, "that I had hoped to have some do what you are doing so that I could make an example of them. But I had no idea that there would be anyone foolish enough to stand up against me and the threat of the furnace—and especially not you." Nebuchadnezzar looked around again as if seeking some counsel from his magistrates and astrologers.

Not a single person opened his mouth.

The cowards didn't dare cross the king.

Outraged by his advisors and by the traitors, Nebuchadnezzar pulled a tuft of hair from his head and held it in his clenched fist. He refused them another chance and ordered the furnace to be heated seven times hotter than usual—referring to it as a death chamber for the first time.

Whispering again to the Jews who bowed around him, Number Four said, "This is exactly what he had hoped. These three are just falling into the king's trap. He wants to burn someone alive to make an example of them."

Jews close by murmured in agreement with Number Four.

Walking away from the king, the guards shook their head as they passed by the Jews in front, saying how it was impossible to heat the furnace to that temperature. "Even if we were able, it would not be possible for any of us to approach it."

"I'm not going to be the one who tells the king that there will be no way to get a prisoner into it, even if we could get it that hot."

"Neither am I," said another, then they immediately ordered some men to bring more fuel.

Number Four's words began to spread like poison as others chimed in. Many of the prostrate Jews quietly whispered among themselves. "These three are not heroes, nor do they possess any common sense. They are nothing but fools." "They could have saved themselves." "What a senseless way to make a point." "It will be upon us now to live for God."

"They will only be remembered for their ignorance," said Number Four. "This proves nothing to the Babylonians about our God."

The murmuring spread like an infection as Jews voiced their cynicism, "The three, like ashes in the wind, will be blown away and remembered no more."

According to Hebrew custom, many of the men ripped their garments in a symbolic gesture of mourning the fate of the condemned brothers, then reverently bowed and prayed.

Hypocrisy.

Nebuchadnezzar stood the entire time with his crown in one hand and hair still clenched in the other. He didn't seem to be bothered by the trickle of blood that ran down the side of his face from where he had torn out the hair. A steely grin cut across his face—lips curling up at the corners.

"Just look at him," said Number Five, jabbing Number Four in the side with an elbow. "It's as if he found some kind of pleasure in making an example of these three."

Indeed, Nebuchadnezzar looked around at his advisors as if seeking accolades.

The bobbing of approving heads stopped abruptly when a messenger reported to the king that the furnace was now too hot to approach.

Swiftly, the king grabbed the sword from a nearby guard. "What!" he shouted, waving the sharp weapon over the heads of those near him in a threatening way. "Drag this traitor away," he said pointing the steel blade back towards the city in the direction of the prison.

Nebuchadnezzar acted more and more like a madman. The tuft of hair scattered into the air when he threw the sword at the owner who managed to dodge the deadly projectile. "Pick that up and take this message to my honor guards," he ordered. "Tell them I want these three Hebrew dogs bound and thrown into the blazing furnace. And if for any reason they think the furnace is too hot to approach then their name will be dishonored. They will share the fate of these three Jews and their legacy will likewise be obliterated in the furnace.

Exploits of the three honor guards had become legendary—exceeding that of the Epic of Gilgamesh. Each one was a commander of one hundred of the best-trained soldiers; together they were famously known and feared as The Three Hundred. During the three years of indoctrination the Jews had heard about them too many times to be counted. Many of the Babylonians believed that the honor guards had descended from the gods. That is why new names of distinction were bestowed upon them. Dagan meant "the exalted one." "Abdi-ili," meant the servant of god, and "Ningirsu," the unrivaled warrior-god. The Babylonians sang songs of their gladiator exploits and spoke of them as if they were immortal.

Upon hearing the command, the honor guards puffed their chests, glanced up at the king, and hastily acted upon their duty. Roughly binding the Jews, the guards showed no sign of mercy on the prisoners nor any apprehension of approaching the fiery furnace.

Number Four rose from his knees briefly and said, "Certainly our God could save us from a madman, but from the fires of Sheol? Let us mourn for our brothers." Withdrawing to his knees, this plea was as far as his courage could take him. Many of the Jews near him nodded in solemn agreement inching together—closing ranks.

Then Nebuchadnezzar was furious with Shadrach, Meshach and Abednego, and his attitude toward them changed. He ordered the furnace heated seven times hotter than usual and commanded some of the strongest soldiers in his army to tie up Shadrach, Meshach and Abednego and throw them into the blazing furnace.[i]

CHAPTER 4

THE TWO

A pitiful group of Jews scuttled together on their knees not far from where Shadrach, Meshach, and Abednego had been led away to the furnace. One of them briefly stood and asked his fellow Jews to mourn for their condemned brothers.

It's not like I hated all of the Jews who had been brought here to live by King Nebuchadnezzar. Having multitudes of foreign captives from the conquered nations doing the menial day-to-day backbreaking labor certainly made life easier for us Babylonians. This also freed the king to use our men for his more important military purposes.

I only despised the privileged captives who got special treatment, who were granted a special diet and were given positions of authority *over those of us* who were *born here*. If it were up to me, I would throw all nine of those Jews who originally defied the orders of the king into the fire. It would serve them right, especially the one who stood up and told others to pray for Shadrach, Meshach, and Abednego. Nothing would please me more than to see him thrown in with the other three.

The king pointed at the satrap I served, snapped his fingers, then pointed at me.

Me, what did I do?

With a push from behind, I was suddenly standing before the king and alongside another low-ranking Babylonian like myself.

"You two will follow closely behind my honor guards and bring back a full report. I am sending you to be my eyewitnesses. You will come back here after the execution and tell me every detail so that it can be recorded by the scribes in the royal annals."

"Yes, your Majesty," said the other Babylonian.

He answered, so I felt it best to keep my mouth shut.

Nebuchadnezzar had his kingdom administration divided into a hierarchy of eight classes of officials. We were the lowest of the low. Daniel, Meshach, Shadrach and Abednego were given higher positions and honor than we were. We were nothing more than errand boys and hated the fact that we had to serve the abhorrent Jews. *It's about time they get what they deserved. Maybe we'll finally get some special recognition by helping out.* It would be my pleasure to bring back every gruesome detail to the king.

Approaching the furnace mound, I shot a glance to the Babylonian beside me as we walked behind the honor guards. I shook my head, and said, "I can feel the heat of the furnace already. There will be no way for the men to approach the fire."

"The king is a madman," my partner whispered to me behind the backs of the famed warriors. I shot a warning look that told him not to let anyone hear what he was saying.

The honor guards kept moving right into the searing heat. By this time, the day was already blistering hot and the weight of their full military regalia must have been unbearable. The lead honor guard, Dagan, paused momentarily to turn his head away from the inferno's heat and wiped the sweat from his eyes.

The second famous soldier pushed Meshach into Dagan from behind—then ducked, hoping to use his prisoner as a shield from the heat. We were only tasked with observing and fell back a couple paces as the honor guards slowed. They pushed the prisoners in front of them and leaned into the blistering hot windstorm.

Then Abdi-ili turned his face away from the blaze and asked Dagan, "Why don't these simple Jews seem bothered by the blaze? After all, they are no better than the weakest Chaldean, let alone a

Babylonian."

Pressing forward, Dagan tucked his head into Shadrach's back and pushed with all of his might. Betraying his name, Dagan was far from exalted when he crouched behind his prisoner. Brown curls of ash that used to be hair, fell from his arms and face.

Ningirsu looked back over his shoulder to the angry king who stood at a safe distance near his throne. Ningirsu steeled himself and plodded forward.

As the god-like warriors approached the opening of the furnace, their clothes steamed as the sweat from their bodies cooked in the dry heat.

We took two more paces back from the fiery heat. No one in their right mind would want to get any closer.

"Look!" said the other Babylonian in horror. "Their skin is burning."

We could not even take the heat from ten paces behind. "These three Babylonian warriors will surely be immortalized forever," I said to my partner—proud of our conquering heritage.

Our faces felt like they were pressed against the sun, even at this distance. Yet, the three guards and their prisoners were much closer. I could see white blisters and the skin on their face begin to blacken—charred by the heat of the fiery flames.

"Push them in and run," Ningirsu said to Dagan. "We'll be worshiped as gods."

"No mortal man could survive this heat...forward," exhorted Abdi-ili. It sounded to me like this was more to himself than to the others.

"Who could approach the sun and live?" Dagan asked.

"Push them in and run," screamed Abdi-ili, who hid behind Abednego. I didn't see any way these three decorated guards could emerge from this unscathed—without being disfigured.

Abdi-ili was the last to reach the furnace. His face was severely charred, yet he had the strength to push Abednego and run. As if Nebo himself breathed fire from his nostrils, the furnace belched and

41

engulfed Abdi-ili in flames. Speechless, the other Babylonian and I looked at each other as the stench of burnt flesh filled our nostrils. Abdi-ili's body lay lifeless in a pile of ashes. I tried to hide my gagging but could not. Abdi-ili had only made it a few steps from the furnace. Repulsed and smelling like smoke, I looked over my shoulder and saw the horrified expression on the faces of the nearby onlookers.

"We can take the report back to the king that the execution is indeed complete," said the other Babylonian, trembling.

Stomach twisted in knots I said nothing and followed him back trying to shake the gruesome memory.

So Shadrach, Meshach and Abednego came out of the fire, and the satraps, prefects, governors and royal advisers crowded around them. They saw that the fire had not harmed their bodies, nor was a hair of their heads singed; their robes were not scorched, and there was no smell of fire on them.[ii]

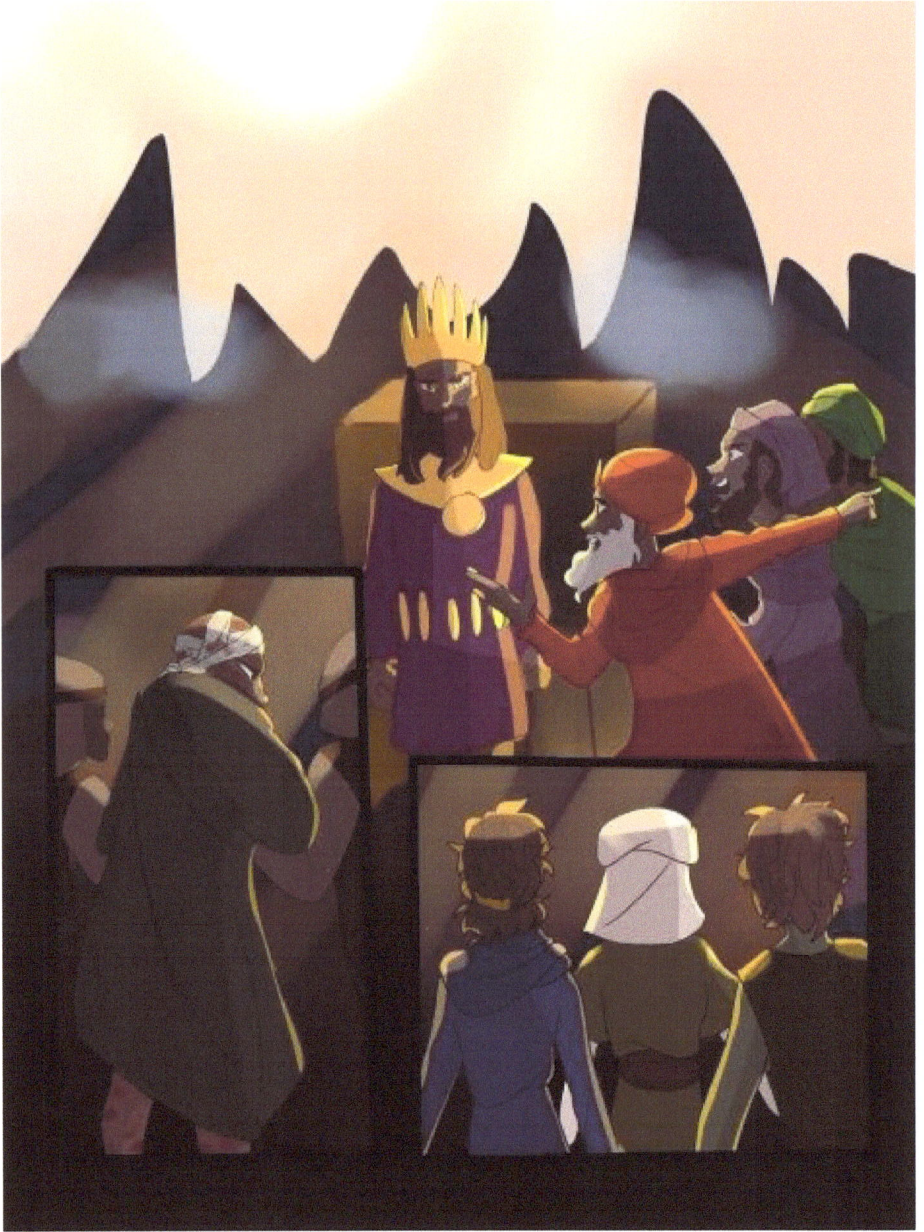

CHAPTER 5

THE ONE

"Look at the king," Number Four said to those around him.

"He stands there like a fool," another one of the privileged Jews said guardedly, while still on his knees near the front.

Degrading the dignity of his office, the king stood with mouth agape, as unmoving as his giant statue. Like someone who had awakened from a bad dream, the king put his face in his hands as if trying to erase a nightmare.

Everything was quiet.

After a long moment, the king tugged upward at the shoulder of his robe and then downward on the material at his waist as if this external straightening could right the inner man.

"Look at him," said Number Seven, "he's trying to act like a king once again."

Ceremoniously, he wiped his hands clean and slapped them together with a gesture of finality. Reaching behind, he grabbed the arms of his ornately carved chair as two satraps rushed to his side assisting him as he sat upon the throne. One whispered something in his ear.

With some pomp, he righted himself and squared his shoulders as if communicating to his subjects that this brutal act sealed his supremacy as unchallenged authority over the world. It was finished.

The test.

The trial.

He had won.

The smile did not last long on his face. It was only a matter of seconds until a clamor broke out, beginning with those closest to the furnace mound. The king looked up from his throne and jumped to his feet. He rubbed his eyes twice and fixed them upon the smelt-turned-death-chamber. There was movement inside.

"Impossible," he yelled and looked in the direction of the two eyewitnesses as if they had answers. The king nearly stumbled off his throne and staggered a few cubits toward the furnace mound.

The Jews in the front whispered among themselves, having no idea what could cause such a reaction.

"Didn't we tie up only three men and throw them into the fire?" the king said, to the two eyewitnesses who had returned.

Dumbfounded, they stood there speechless.

As he moved forward, the people parted before him. It was not out of respect for the king but more like they knew they were witness to something of even greater importance. The noisy rumblings of the multitudes became so quiet that it was possible to hear the slap of the king's sandals on the hard-packed dirt.

Drawing closer, the king stopped again. "Look! I see four men walking around in the fire. They are not tied up, and they are not burned," the king said. "The…the…*the* fourth man looks like a son of the gods. Shadrach, Meshach, and Abednego come out!" He yelled, visibly shaking—wiping tears from his face. "Servants of the Most High God, come here."

Nebuchadnezzar did not seem the least bit concerned about the cheers of the Jews who began praising God.

"God has done it," said a member of the elite Jews, "just as Shadrach had said."

"The Lord has saved Shadrach, Meshach, and Abednego."

Number Four mumbled something under his breath.

When the three men stepped out of the fire, the multitudes gasped. The governors, the prefects, the royal advisers and the two observers pressed in around them. "Look," said one of the eyewitnesses, "not even one hair on their body was burned by the flames."

Assisted by a man under each arm, Dagan limped over to see. "How could this be?" said the disfigured warrior in astonishment. Dagan had been draped in a cloth to hide his scarred and ugly nakedness—his garments burned away and armor melted.

"And look," shouted one of the king's advisors, who darted glances back and forth between Dagan and the three Jews, "their clothes are in perfect condition—"

"And they don't even smell like smoke," screamed one of the astrologers, waving his hands in the air, bewildered by the contrast.

Nebuchadnezzar hushed the outburst by raising his hand.

Part 3

FAILURE

CHAPTER 6

THE SHAME

Stunned silence soon quelled the rancor of the multitudes.

"Praise the God of Shadrach, Meshach, and Abednego," Nebuchadnezzar shouted, then turned to address the crowd. "Their God has sent His angel and saved His servants from the fire. These three men trusted their God and refused to obey my command. They were willing to die rather than serve or worship any god other than their own. So I now give a new decree. Anyone from any nation or language who says anything against the God of Shadrach, Meshach, and Abednego will be torn apart and have his house turned into a pile of stones. No other god can save his people like this."

Many of the Jews cheered the king's words as Number Four jabbed the Jew next to him with a sharp elbow. "The God of Shadrach, Meshach, and Abednego?" he said mimicking the king. "This is our God, too. Who do they think they are?"

"Yeah," said the fellow as he rubbed his ribs, "we knew God could save us. It would not have been practical for all of us to have to prove it."

"We would have if it came down to it," said another near the front, balefully.

"Yes, but those three refused to let practicality get in the way of

51

their faith," said one of the Jews at the top of his voice, in a condemning tone.

Turning around with furrowed brow, Number Four shouted back to the less privileged Jew, "I was willing to die, but it would have been meaningless. As someone already said, it didn't take more than these three to prove *our* point."

"The example of faith and bravery of these three changed the king's heart while I bowed down to a lifeless god. You call that meaningless?" yelled out the lower-class Jew.

The king spoke again which silenced the Jews.

"Scribes, what I have already spoken shall be written. No other god can save his people like the God of Shadrach, Meshach and Abednego and nothing is to be said against them," shouted the king.

Number Four pushed forward, grabbed the shoulders of the two men in front of him, hoisted himself up on tiptoe, and said to the king, "He is our God and He could have saved us too."

Foolish.

Number Five and Number Six wormed their way through the crowd and stood shoulder to shoulder with Number Four.

"Look how brave they are now," said a Jew, rising to his feet and brushing the dust from his garments.

The three pressed forward but didn't get very far before being barred by a sentry. "How dare you approach the king?"

Number Four shouted over those in front of him. "We demand to take a stand for our God."

"You already had your chance to prove your trust in the Lord, but came up lacking," said a brother who was still on his knees.

"Get out of the way," Number Four said to the stone-faced sentry, spitting out his words as if trying to remove the taste of bitter herbs from his mouth. "I want to address the king."

Another Jew grabbed Number Four from behind, pleading with him to stop. "Men, no doubt you have enough faith to believe in God like the rest of us, but just like me, you did not have enough faith to burn for God. Let it be."

"Well, we shall see about that," said one of the three emboldened Jews.

The pushing and shoving caught the king's attention. "What is the meaning of this?"

The officer of the guard released his restraining grip, turned, and bowed before the king. "These three princes of Judah you have chosen as provincial officials demand an audience with His Majesty."

The guard and the three in his charge waited while the king convened with Abednego, Meshach, and Shadrach.

With a wave of his hand, the king signaled for the guard to bring the three Jews forward.

Standing before the king and brushing the dust from his fine Babylonian garments Number Four addressed the king. "We too believe in the Most High God—"

"Men," the king interrupted, "dignity is not something you wear or put on the outside, it must come from within like Meshach, Abednego, and Shadrach."

"We, too, stood, O king."

"You may have stood, but you did not stand long enough—"

"But—"

"Dare to interrupt me?"

Bowing. "Apologies my king, but…but we wish to make a stand now," said Number Four.

The king turned to Shadrach, Meshach, and Abednego.

They nodded to the king.

"Hananiah? Mishael? I mean…Shadrach and Meshach?" Number Four pleaded.

The king turned to his right and extended his hand for Meshach to speak.

"We told the king to hear you out and to answer according to the things he has learned this day." Finishing his words, Meshach turned back to the king and conceded with a respectful bow.

"What is it that you want?" snapped the king with an air of impatience.

"We demand to be thrown into the fire."

The folly of pride. The worst of masters.

Without looking to his left where his astrologers, sorcerers, and enchanters stood as advisors, the king instead looked over to the three faithful Jews on his right.

The three looked to each other, and again, Shadrach nodded to the king as if having complete confidence he would do the right thing.

With narrowed eyes, the king peered at the Jews who had pushed their way up front and gave orders. "Guards, you have heard these *brave* Jews who stepped forward and asked to be thrown into the fire. Bind them and heat the furnace."

Stepping towards the king, Shadrach stopped in his tracks when Nebuchadnezzar held up his hand. "What I have said, I have said."

As the furnace heated up, two of the bound Jews fell to their knees. "O king, I repent. This was only a show to hide my cowardice," said one.

"We were ashamed of our actions and felt we could make up for it like this," said the other looking up to Shadrach, Meshach, and Abednego. "Pride got us here, not faith—may the Lord forgive us."

"What about you?" the king asked Number Four.

"I have as much faith as Shadrach, Meshach, and Abednego and will prove it," said Number Four, unyielding. "If you throw me into the blazing furnace, the God I serve is able to deliver me from it and from Your Majesty's hand." Number Four turned to the Jews within hearing distance and said, "Nebuchadnezzar, I will not serve your gods or worship the image of gold you have set up."

It was pitiful.

With sharp words, Nebuchadnezzar gave orders. "Unbind those two and return them to the rest of the captives. They are not fit for service to the king."

A messenger approached the king and reported that the furnace was now seven times hotter as he had commanded.

"Do you want to bow?" the king asked Number Four.

Standing tall, the proud Jew did not open his mouth and extended his bound hands in a gesture that expressed that he was ready to be led away to the furnace.

"Guards, seize this man," ordered Nebuchadnezzar with sternness in his voice. "Stand him before me." With no more than a cubit's distance between them, the king sized him up from head to toe and then said, "I will not question your faith in the One True God. I do, however, question how great is that faith—"

Number Four stood like a statue, despite the judging tone of Nebuchadnezzar's accusation.

For a long moment, the only sound was the roar of the flames.

The king finished by saying, "I'm not sure your faith is such that you deserve to burn for your God."

Number Four closed his eyes, slumped his shoulders and placed his face in his bound hands.

The shame.

"Carry this one to the hills…leagues outside the city and unbind him."

Shadrach loosened his tense shoulders, exhaled, and said, "You have acted wisely, O king."

The king responded humbly, "It is not wisdom that I claim as my own. The vanity in my heart has been changed by your faith. I deserve no credit and only hope to please the God of Shadrach, Meshach, and Abednego."

Shadrach gave a dignified bow to the king then turned and watched Number Four being led away in solemn procession.

"Blessed be the God of Shadrach, Meshach and Abednego," said the king.

As for me, I shall not put my name to this letter, I am undeserving of my Hebrew name.

For I was Number Four.

Part 4

FORGIVENESS

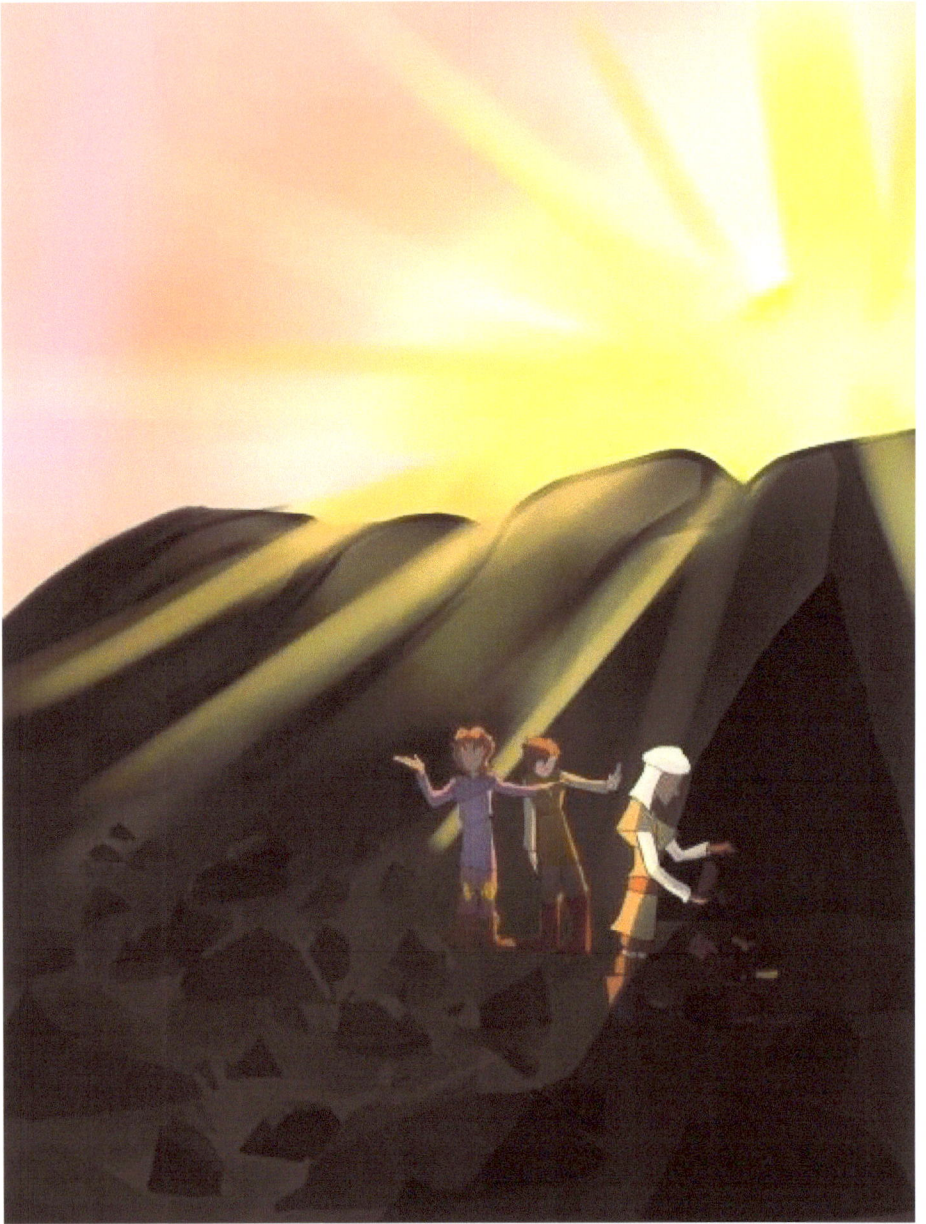

CHAPTER 7

THE GIFT

Even though free from Nebuchadnezzar's rule, my cowardice did not allow me any celebration of that liberty. Banished far from the city I was confined by the prison walls of guilt.

I would have gladly lived out the rest of my days without any name—Jewish or Babylonian. To live in the filth of this dark cave is what I deserved. To be exiled and alone is the destiny I merited. God has no place for faithless people like me and has chosen me for wrath. Suffering the furnace would have been better than this searing pain of shame; death better than the imprisonment of disgrace.

After more than a year of searching, Shadrach, Meshach, and Abednego found me in a dirt hollow in the hills of Kish—near death from starvation. They refused to leave when I told them to go. Humiliated by my sin, I explained that their faith changed a nation, while my lack of faith exposed my pride and hurt the reputation of God's holy name. "I can never lift my eyes higher than the hills again," I said.

They assured me that not everyone is called by God to walk through fire. They made a strong case for God's faithfulness despite our faithlessness. "God is not glorified in disobedience," Abednego pointed out, but said that I did not have to walk through the fire to prove anything to Him.

Meshach spoke of God's forgiveness.

I fell to my knees and wept. "How can it be? I let my pride get the best of me. I was such a fool" I tried to explain through tears. "Not me."

"Yes you," said Abednego.

"My sin is too great." I argued.

"His love knows no bounds."

"Impossible. That would be scandalous," I told them. "God could not love a person like me."

"That's exactly what it is," Meshach told me, "beautiful scandalous grace."

I cried even harder. Shadrach put his hand under my chin and lifted my face upward. These three messengers did better than give me back my Babylonian name—they gave me a new Hebrew name.

"You shall be called Meshullam."

"It means, 'Paid For,'" said Meshach.

"It also means 'Friend,'" Abednego said, assisting me to my feet. "Your help comes from beyond the mountains, from the Maker of heaven and earth."[iii]

They were the first words of scripture I had heard in over a year. I closed my eyes and breathed it in. A psalm that warmed my heart and soothed my pain like a healing salve.

Meshullam might not be the best of Hebrew names, but the name I needed. God was merciful in not giving me what I deserved and gracious in pursuing me with love I did not earn. God does not set aside righteous judgments. He owes us nothing but judgment for our sin. It is only by understanding what we owe and by putting our trust in Him to be our salvation can we experience His mercy.

I desperately wanted to become something. I had a childhood dream of greatness. I wanted to be known like Shadrach, Meshach, and Abednego but my name will be blotted from this story. It took the gift of brokenness for me to understand that I belong to Him—that He knows my name. I take comfort knowing that He accepts me despite my failure and regardless of what others think about me.

What a great God.

———————— 🔥 ————————

Years later, after Cyrus the Great of Persia conquered Babylon and let our people go back to Jerusalem I decided to stay behind with Daniel. After hearing from Jeremiah and studying the prophets, I realized that although we were sent here as a judgment on us, God had divine plans for us while here in exile. Ezekiel wrote that it was for God's sake that He scattered us among the nations. The world would come to know that He is Lord when He shows himself holy through us.[iv]

No one wanted to listen to Jeremiah when he said that God carried us here to build houses and plant crops and said that we should pray for the peace and prosperity of Babylon.[v] I discovered that as God's people He had a purpose for us while we were here.

In the way that Shadrach, Meshach, and Abednego had been sent to me as messengers of God's grace we were sent by Him to be His witness nation to those outside Judah. We had refused to go, believing that we were the ends of God's grace not the means of His grace. In God's covenant with Abraham, we have been blessed by Him to be a blessing to all nations.[vi] Yet, I realize that by nature we are a stubborn and hard-hearted people, selfishly trying to keep His blessings to ourselves.

As I have had time to search Scripture, it has become clear to me for the first, time that God has a sending attribute to His nature. We don't go because it is in our nature to do so, instead, we go because it is God's nature to send.[vii] Isaiah wrote, "Then I heard the voice of the Lord saying, "Whom shall I send? And who will go for us?"" It was God who put us here for His purposes.

I may not have walked through the fire, but I have since prayed for the faith of Shadrach, Meshach, and Abednego and the strength that comes only from God to say, "Here am I LORD. Send me!" like Isaiah responded.[viii] I knew in His sovereignty, He had carried me and put me here in this spot. He has called me to be a blessing to the people and in the culture around me for the sake of His holy name and that His glory would extend beyond the walls of Jerusalem—to all tongues, tribes, and nations.[ix]

———————— ✦ ————————

Later, when retelling the story of the fiery furnace to the younger Jews in Babylon I discovered something new. As I recited the story in the language of our homeland, God's story unfolded before me in a way I had never seen. The Hebrew names of these heroes of faith spoken aloud were the story. The Babylonian names of Shadrach, Meshach and Abednego meant nothing to me; however, by His divine orchestration, the names Hananiah, Mishael, and Azariah prove to be a powerful message about the character of God.

Repeating these names over and over struck me again. As on the day of my rescue, I fell to my knees and wept, worshipping God as if a glorious symphony burst forth from the heavens.

The name Hananiah is "Jehovah has been gracious." Mishael is Hebrew for, "Who is like God?" And it is no mere coincidence that Azariah means "Jehovah has helped."

Jehovah has been gracious.

Who is like God?

Jehovah has helped.

It had been in front of us the entire time. The story about the three Jews who would not bow down was the unfolding drama of God's glory—this is about Him. He had been gracious. There is no other like Him. As He stepped down into the fire for Shadrach, Meshach, and Abednego we can trust Him to be our help in time of need. Recounting the events and rehearsing those names brought me great joy.

"Certainly these men of faith are worth emulating, but don't be distracted by them." I told the children. "Look beyond them and there you'll see the greatness of God."

Mercy triumphs over judgment, because *Jehovah is gracious.*

God is worth living and dying for, because *Who is like God?*

We can overcome every temptation because *Jehovah has helped*.

It is not by my power or might, but only in the strength He provides. I had tried on the merits of my own self-determination and failed miserably.

It was He who *paid* my ransom so I could be set free and called a *friend* of God. His mercy does not dispense with judgment, but triumphs over the judgment we deserve. Lifting my hands heavenwards, I looked up as if being refreshed in the cleansing water of grace like rain.

Grace.

Forgiveness.

Redemption.

Hope

All four are a free gift to those who put their trust in God, our Savior. He has proven Himself faithful in His promise to restore our people to Jerusalem. Therefore, He can be trusted to fulfill His promise of sending a Redeemer—the coming King.

I was not respected by the Babylonians but thankfully, Daniel still had tremendous influence here. With great attentiveness, a wealthy, priestly sect of diviners eagerly searched the Law and Prophets regarding Messiah, yet mixed the truth with their preoccupation of astrology and astronomy. Known as the Magi, they were of the highest class of officials within Nebuchadnezzar's hierarchy and answered only to Daniel, as the "chief administrator over all the wise men of Babylon."[x]

I shall now sign my name to this letter not because of who I am, but because of what God has done. It is not because of what I have done, but because of Who God Is.

Sincerely,

Meshullam

A *Friend* Who Has Been *Paid For*.

MARK DAHLIN

The Lord bless you
and keep you;
the Lord make his face shine on you
and be gracious to you;
the Lord turn his face toward you
and give you peace.[xi]

ABOUT THE AUTHOR

MARK DAHLIN is founder of Dead Reckoning Ministries, adjunct professor of Biblical Studies at Epic Bible College and Graduate School in Sacramento, and pastor at Living Hope Church in Roseville, California. Mark is happily married to an avid artist, Kerry. They live in Citrus Heights, have four incredible adult children and two grandchildren.
You can find his videos on YouTube
and follow his **Dead Reckoning Ministries** on Facebook.

For speaking engagements, retreats, seminars, books or Bible Study materials, Mark may be contacted directly at **markdahlin@yahoo.com**

Mark shares his hilarious and unbelievable childhood stories at **markdahlin.blogspot.com**. His blog, read in over 100 countries around the world, is the online journal of his quest to find meaning and connection.

i   Dan 3:19-20
ii   Dan 3:26b-27
iii   Psalm 121:1-2
iv   Ezekiel 36:22-23
v   Jer 29:4-11
vi   Gen 12:2-3; 18:18; Zech 8:18-23; Acts 3:25
vii   Malachi 3:1; John 20:21; Matt 4:19; Matt 10:40; Matt 28:19-20; Mark 16:15
viii   Isaiah 6:8
ix   Invited by God, empowered, gifted and perfectly positioned for the *Missio Dei*—the Mission of God.
x   Dan 2:48
xi   Num 6:24-26

www.ingramcontent.com/pod-product-compliance
Lightning Source LLC
LaVergne TN
LVHW010028070426
835513LV00001B/8